NASTY ASTROLOGY

NASTY ASTROLOGY

What your astrologer won't tell you about your star sign

Richard MacDonald

COLLINS & BROWN

First published in Great Britain in 2004
by Collins & Brown Limited
The Chrysalis Building
Bramley Road
London W10 6SP

An imprint of **Chrysalis** Books Group plc

Distributed in the United States and Canada by Sterling
Publishing Co., 387 Park Avenue South, New York, NY 10016,
USA

3 5 7 9 8 6 4

British Library Cataloguing-in-Publication Data: A catalogue
record for this book is available from the British Library.

ISBN 1 84340 133 9

Designed by Gemma Wilson
Project managed by Miranda Sessions
Illustrated by Tania Field

Reproduction by Anorax Imaging, UK.
Printed and bound by Times Offset, Malaysia.

CONTENTS

Introduction

Aren't you bored with all the astrology books that tell you what a nice person everyone is? Don't you know, deep down, that there are some very unpleasant aspects to all our characters? Wouldn't you like to know the truth about the other signs? What makes them tick? What their dirty dark little secrets are?

✷ find out exactly what hidden demons lurk within other people's psyches

Well now you can. In this wonderfully nasty book you can find out exactly what hidden demons lurk within other people's psyches, and learn about the personalities of your friends and lovers, boss and

colleagues – not to mention the nasty vices of your own sign. This book lifts the lid on real astrology – and dares to tell the truth. You'll know exactly how everybody around you really thinks and feels – and what could you do with such valuable information?

This isn't really a book to give to your friends – keep it for yourself. Read about the secrets that motivate others – but never read the bits about yourself. You will quickly learn how to use this information to your advantage; how to push other people's buttons, seduce them, win money at cards from them, get them to clean up after you, cook for you and generally become your slave.

✳ Read about the
secrets that
motivate others – but
never read the bits
about yourself

7

Each sign is divided up into five sections – an introduction, personality, love, sex and business. You'll soon learn what each sign is like when they fall in love, what they are like in bed and how they earn their money.

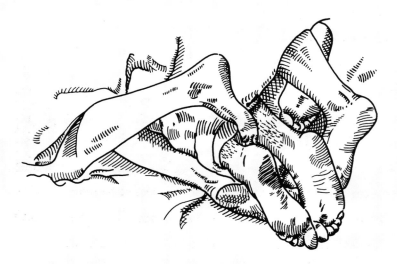

✳ Turn to your lover's sign and see what makes them tick

Once again, please do not read your own sign. I know it is tempting – especially for Aries, pushy little devils – but resist the urge to turn to your own first. Instead turn to your lover's sign and see what makes them tick. Have a look at your employer's, that'll teach 'em to be horrid to you. Look up your friends, you'll see what they really think of the world.

Each section contains the real them, the person behind closed doors, the bits they never let you see. In the outside world we all wear a mask, but at home, on our own, in private, we take that mask off and what is revealed is worse than any Phantom of any opera. What you will find is the skull grinning, the

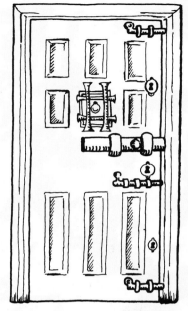

monster unveiled, the deepest darkest secret us that we reveal to no one. Yuck, quite horrid. I say, don't read your own sign. You'd never believe it anyway. You'd never believe that you could be revealed in all your glorious nastiness, that some one had peeped behind the mask and seen you without your makeup, unshaven, unwashed, unclean, undressed. What a revolting thought.

Have fun.

Richard MacDonald.

Aries

Taurus

Cancer

Gemini

Aquarius

Virgo

Sagittarius

Caprico

the Signs

Libra

Scorpio

Leo

Pisces

Aries

22nd March — 20th April

Arians are independent and hold most people in contempt.
They have a quick fiery temper and are impatient and scornful
of advice. They can be exceedingly abrupt and blunt. Their
arrogance knows no bounds. They think there are only two
ways to do anything – their way and the wrong way. They
may be right, but they lack diplomatic skills and will win no
friends. When it comes to relationships and commitment they
are still looking for the meaningful one-night-stand. They're
not as tall as they say they are.

Personality

> *They like to think they are brave, that they are great leaders. If they would hold up for long enough to look behind them they would see no one is following. If you catch them unawares in the bathroom they'll be acting out speeches or practising being interviewed on chat shows. They are vain and big-headed and egotistic and over-confident. Prick their fragile bubbles, though, and they'll cry like babies. They have no staying power, no stamina for a fight, no resistance and no reserves. They are weak and would willingly bribe their way out of any trouble.*

✱ *If you catch them unawares in the bathroom, they'll be acting out speeches or practising being interviewed on chat shows*

In any real risky situation you'll find them leading from the back. Once the excitement and danger is over they will become very vocal about their achievements and success on the field – how very brave they were, and how the whole battle would have been lost if they hadn't saved the day at the last moment, by the skin of their teeth. This is, of course, a complete fiction.

> *They think they look slimmer than they are. They are always planning to enrol on a martial arts course. They never do. They run to seed and grow fat.*

They think the whole of life is like a gigantic game of chess – they play to win and they play to make you lose. There is no other outcome as far as they are concerned – and your losing is as important, if not more so, than their winning.

They do like to gamble – with your affections, with the law, with their very lives. You'd be better off having nothing to do with them in case they drag you down with them into the bankruptcy courts, the pits, even into hell itself.

✳ *They think the whole of life is like a gigantic game of chess – they play to win and they play to make you lose*

They are unbelievably competitive and will turn anything into a bet, a competition, a race, a wager, a gamble, a contest, a fight. Put them under any real pressure, though, and they'll cave in. They'll do anything to win and will resort to trickery, fraud, lying and good old-fashioned cheating. This applies to any situation – relationships, business, love and friendships.

They grow into grumpy old men and sour old women. Mind you, they start out pretty grumpy – but it only reaches a climax when they are old and think they can get away

with it. They are lazy, self-indulgent, corrupt and avaricious
– and that's the good side of them.

> *They are lazy, self-indulgent, corrupt and avaricious – and that's the good side of them*

Aries people will never ask for help as they think they
can cope just fine on their own. They will, however, always
take over anyone else's tasks as they think they can do
everything better than anyone else. If they would slow down
for a moment that might be true – unlikely but true.

Aries in love

God but the Aries do like to fall in love. It's something they
do at the drop of a hat – or a pair of briefs. They keep their
hearts in their pants, so it is easy to get an Aries to fall in
love with you – just sleep with them. They are, however,
puppy-like in love, and will follow their intended around
with hang-dog expressions, flowers and lust in their eyes.
They stay in love long after all traces of love have
evaporated. It takes dynamite to shift them. You can try
being as nasty as you like, and they'll still follow you
around. They can never quite believe that anyone could
stop loving them despite their unlovable natures. Tangle
with them at your peril. They are like limpets, clinging to
your knees as you try to leave them.

> *They can never quite believe that anyone could stop loving them*

They are completely unreliable in love and will be swearing undying devotion while trying to seduce your sister, your brother, or both. They come across as curiously old-fashioned but they have the morals of a mongoose. They like to buy flowers and small cheap gifts, but only in an attempt to get you into bed.

They'll take you to a Greek island – as long as they can get cheap flights – and spend the whole time trying to have a holiday romance under your very nose.

Aries and sex

Morals of a mongoose? Ha! The mongoose society would have them thrown out for lax morals. They would sleep with anything that moves, given half a chance. They think fidelity is not thinking of someone else while they're with you. The kinkier it is the more likely you are to find Aries there with their noses in the trough. If it involves leather, whips, pain, humiliation and degradation – it'll be too tame for them.

If it involves leather, whips, pain, humiliation and degradation – it'll be too tame for them.

They are always dreaming of three-in-a-bed sessions, but both of their sex partners would have to be in love with them, and not with each other – the Aries couldn't stand that. They also like the idea of sex in public – but only the idea; they are actually quite prudish and wouldn't even let you kiss them in the open. For all their talk of kinky sex, they are very conventional in bed.

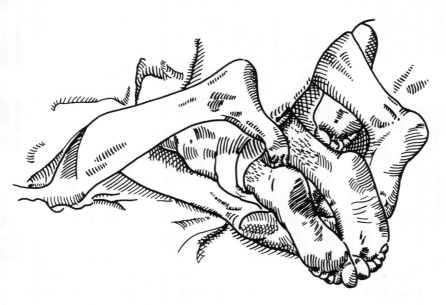

They like the idea of lots of regular sex but if they get it they get bored, so keep them guessing, keep them wanting more, keep them at arms length if you ask me. They think they've got unbelievably high libidos but they cool quickly if they get too much. They are passionately jealous and make dangerous love rivals – they'll play dirty to get exactly what they want, so watch out. They think they look good in the nude. They don't.

Aries in business

They are bossy and controlling, domineering and egotistical. They think they are right, infallible, untouchable, perfect, fool-proof and terribly cuddly. Tell them they are arrogant and bossy and they won't have a clue what you are talking about. They think they are caring, supportive and kind and thoughtful. That shows you how out of touch with themselves they are.

If they work for others they are uppity, unhelpful, lazy, and will cheerfully steal your ideas and claim them as their own. They use the office as a place for seduction, corruption and sleep and will happily claim unfair dismissal if they get caught. They will gossip and cause trouble if you don't keep an eye on them permanently.

✳ They use the office as a place for seduction, corruption and sleep

If they work for themselves they either go bankrupt or make a fortune – nothing in-between for them. They think they work hard – and will tell you this constantly – but in reality they skive and shirk their duties. They think they are 'ideas' people but most of their best ideas are stolen from others.

If they do get rich they'll hoard the money and still buy you cheap gifts. Their idea of a Christmas bonus for their staff is Boxing day off. Their idea of a Christmas bonus for themselves is a racing car. They also like to reuse last year's Christmas cards, and will ask people to sign them in pencil so they can be re-cycled.

taurus

21st April – 21 May

Taureans like others to think of them as refined, and experts when it comes to food and drink. This is just a cover; they are in reality a glutton and a drunk. They care nothing for culture, it's all a matter of getting quantity rather than quality, although they do make a good job of fooling most people. They are greedy both for oral satisfaction and material wealth. No one can accumulate quite like them. They can also do a nice line in fake environmental concern – they really couldn't give a damn just so long as they own it all. They have too many close relatives.

Personality

Hey, don't cross these babies. They have horns and spikes and all sorts of weapons. They probably sleep with shotguns under the bed. They are quick to lose their temper. They like to throw tantrums to get their own way and will carry on doing so long after childhood has left them behind. If they can't get their own way they'll attack you. Cross them at your peril.

They like to think of themselves as oak trees with their roots firmly entrenched in the soil of their earth. Yes, they are like oak trees; unable to move, easy to get struck down in storms, big, ugly, strong and stupid.

They feel threatened a lot – so tend to barricade themselves in behind security devices, barbed wire, gun turrets and arrow slits. They think everyone is out to rob them. We are.

✱ They think everyone is out to rob them. We are

They often come across as ruddy-faced, cheerful and slightly drunk old buffoons – think Falstaff, think Santa Claus, think Duke Ellington. But they are never as casual and laid back as they appear. Think instead of a shrewd operator, think of a canny business person, think acting and pretence. They like you to think of them as silly, but beneath that bluff exterior beats a heart of solid dollar signs.

✳ think Falstaff, think Santa Claus, think Duke Ellington

Don't ever ask one of them what they think. For a start they'll tell you and tell you in blunt, plain old fashioned words. Boy, do they have a mouth on them. They like to use foul language – they think it makes them more likable and earthy. The truth is they are just foul – and they like to drone on endlessly once asked. Don't give them the opportunity. Shut them up or they'll bore you forever. They could bore for their country.

> *They don't like to be rushed and they don't like to take risks. Oh, you think those qualities are admirable? Then you must be one of them and you were told not to read this. The rest of us – the other eleven signs – find them slow and cowardly. They can't be hurried – or won't – and they are so frightened of risking a dollar they'd rather lose a thousand than take the risk. They get cuckolded a lot.*

Taureans are so rich it's worth the effort of stealing from them. Other signs are poor, so not worth bothering with, but a Taurus will always reward you with rich pickings. They

know this and hide
their stuff away
– it's always
under the bed
by the way.
They have too
many books.

Taurus in love

Can you imagine the
lengths they'd go to,
to avoid falling in love?
Love is soppy, messy,
risky, time-consuming.
They'd much rather be
eating or drinking or
hoarding money. Being in love
means outlay – you have to buy a ring,
flowers, wine, a honeymoon, a wedding, anniversary cards.

✳ They'd much rather be eating or
drinking or hoarding money

Once they do fall in love you'd better hope it ain't you.
They will stifle you, lock you away, smother you with tacky
gifts, suffocate you with attention and affection. They think
having lots of children will keep them safe from being
dumped. They have a particularly claustrophobic approach
to long-term relationships – you aren't allowed out of their
sight. Instinctively they know they're going to get dumped
eventually and they try everything to prevent it – which

brings it on all the quicker. They hate to be betrayed and will get so angry and put on such a show of indignation – 'How could you do this to me?' they'll bellow. Brilliant fun to goad one.

> *But if you do betray one stay well out of their way, as they are very violent when aroused, and are likely to commit murder – or assault at the very least. You wouldn't want one of these as a real enemy.*

Taurus and sex

They do like to plot a seduction though and will ponderously go about it. But finesse, charm, grace? No, these are not words they will be familiar with. Exaggerated, theatrical, overexcited, now that's more like it. Think bulls rutting. Think cows being mounted. Think bovine. Think big. Think ungainly. Think all over in a second.

✱ Think bovine. Think big. Think ungainly. Think all over in a second

They don't like to be thwarted in their love interests and will pursue somebody long after they've been given a clear message to back off. They don't take hints so you will have to give them the brush-off with real brushes, or boots. They are immune to subtlety so you will have to spell it out to them in simple words: 'Go away, I don't want to sleep with you, you are repugnant'. There, that should do it, hopefully, but it might be a bit too understated for them.

✳ 'Go away, I don't want to sleep with you, you are repugnant'

> *Their sexual preferences tend towards the natural, the basic, the lusty and the rude. They don't like kinky sex – they are afraid it might cost them too much. They like quick, no-nonsense sex, to be got over with as quickly as possible so that they can have a cream tea.*

They don't like to change partners too often, as breaking in a new lover takes too much time, too much money, too much effort. They are so lazy that they would stick with someone pretty well no matter what, rather than have to go looking for a new lover.

Taureans in business

Basically they are quite honest – good to be able to say something nice – but they will try every trick in the book to get one over on you, when it comes to finances. Once the deal is struck – and it will be on their terms believe me – they'll stick to it through thick and thin. Unflinching loyalty is their strong point – their only one – and they do like to milk it – 'Call me Honest John', that sort of thing. But in all seriousness do you know what the ideal occupation is for a Taurean? I'll tell you – Estate Agent. Yes, that's how bad it gets. At best? A wine merchant.

They all think they can be gardeners, farmers, horticulturists – what nonsense. There's not a green finger amongst them. They think they're good in the country but the suburbs is the place for them – all lace curtains and three-piece suites. They like to think they've got good taste but it is firmly set in the 1950's.

★ what is the ideal occupation for a Taurean? I'll tell you – Estate Agent. Yes, that's how bad it gets

Working for themselves is not for them. They like a wage packet too much. And a pension scheme and bonus schemes and loyalty bonuses – getting the message? Yep, they like bonuses. I wouldn't employ one, they're such sticklers for details, far too bogged down in petty rules and bureaucracy. They don't have a lot of initiative. They also steal pens.

Gemini

22 May – 21 June

*For a Gemini, life is just one long game. It has no reality –
they see it all as a movie or a computer game. They are good
at business but shouldn't be trusted near others' piggy banks,
pocket money or purses. They'll steal and lie and cheat – just so
long as they look good and appear on top. They have no morals,
no ethics and will reach the top. They'd sell their granny if they
could make money on her.*

Personality

*What quality do you think they value above all others?
Cunning, that's what. Not a very nice thing to live your life
by, is it? But that's what motivates them, what gets them out
of bed. Offer them an honest $100 and they'd turn it down for
the crooked $10. They like to think they've managed to trick
you, to sell you faulty goods. They are more crooked than you'd
ever believe.*

They also like to talk about themselves rather too much.
Because they all suffer from split-personalities, there are two
of each of them to bore you to death with all the details of
their cons and tricks and swindles and merry japes. They
think all the stunts they've pulled off make them somehow
more attractive, charming, alluring. Instead it makes them
seem thin and mean and callous. They make good bar room
lawyers.

You'll often find Gemini in exotic places where it suits
their mood exactly – modern, loud, dangerous, open to deals
being struck. They are restless people and often end up
living abroad – mainly to escape the tax, the police, the
landlord, people they've conned or abused or upset.

✝ Because they all suffer from
split-personalities there are two of
each of them to bore you to death

Bouncy. That pretty well sums them up. Always on
the move. Always selling, plotting, planning, scheming.
The reason? They're too afraid to sit still for long in case

the world catches up with them – or themselves. They are frightened of the big stuff, the deep stuff – which is why they spend their lives on the trivia – the buying and the selling. Oh yes, and the surfing (real or cyber) and any outdoor pursuits.

✳ **Too afraid to sit still for long in case the world catches up with them.**

They live on their nerves and their superficiality. They are shallow little beasts and only care about turning a dollar, making a buck, earning a bob or two – and even, if necessary, picking a pocket or two. Strangely, however, they do have a curious code of ethics, a sort of burglars code or criminals charter whereby they do apply certain principles to their antics. For instance, they would never rob a granny – sell their own granny of course – but never rob one.

✳ **They live on their nerves and their superficiality**

You can't shut them up or turn them off or turn them down. They are full on, in your face, never sleeping, never backing off. They are lively, inquisitive, and almost rodent-like. All their siblings leave home before them. They hate injustice – perceived or real – and will make a great nuisance of themselves writing to newspapers about unintended slights perpetrated on them by shop workers, garage forecourt assistants and police officers. They suffer a permanent persecution complex. They deserve to be persecuted.

Gemini in love

When the Gemini falls in love doesn't everybody have to hear about it. *And* all the gory details – 'he said this, she did that'. It's enough to make you sick. Why can't they keep it all to themselves? When they get dumped you'd think the world had ended. The sad thing is, it seems to happen so often, so regularly, you'd think they'd either get used to it or have a look at why it happens so much.

✱ When they get dumped you'd think the world had ended

They do like to dominate in a relationship. Any partner is in for a cruel awakening when they realize they are going to play second fiddle to a jumped up little dictator. Then they're usually out of there pretty quick, leaving behind a broken-hearted Gemini crying twice as loud and twice as long. Before too long they've had as many lovers as a Swiss Army knife has blades.

> *Don't expect them to read books about relationships, they don't see any need to change anything – it's always somebody else's fault. They don't read any books actually.*

✱ **They've had as many lovers as a Swiss Army Knife has blades**

Gemini and sex

Think prude. Think old-fashioned. Think holding hands. Its all a bit boring, a bit sad, and a bit wet. They can lose lovers through their lack of attention to the body bits. They like to think they're faithful, and according to their own curious code of conduct they are. God help their partner if they stray though. All hell would break loose around them.

No one betrays a Gemini and gets off without a sound ear-bashing. But that's as far as it goes. They rant and shout but they aren't violent. They're too scared.

✳ *No one betrays a Gemini and gets off without a sound ear-bashing*

Gemini in business

They sell cars. They sell toasters. They sell carpets. They sell anything to anybody, anytime, anywhere. They love to sell. Just as long as they feel they are getting one over on you they are happy. Whatever you do don't employ one. They will steal the office furniture out from underneath you – and then sell it back to you. They have no scruples in business.

In business they are happy as long as they can talk – and they can talk the proverbial hind-leg off a donkey – and they will talk to anyone about anything, and all of it is pure gibberish, total nonsense. They invariably have no qualifications for the job they do – they will have talked their way in of course. They feel they have something to prove all the time. The weight of the chip on the shoulder is enormous.

✳ *Whatever you do don't employ one. They will steal the office furniture out from underneath you*

> If they work for anyone else they will cause trouble. They
> always think they know how to do your job better than you do
> and they will stir up feelings of negativity and discontent in the
> workplace.

*They break everything eventually
as they can't stop fiddling*

Intellectually they are a bit lightweight, a bit trivial, a bit slender, so don't give them anything taxing to do or anything requiring research or the use of a computer – they'll only break it. They break everything eventually, as they can't stop fiddling. As children they broke all their toys, blamed their siblings, and then claimed they weren't loved as they had nothing to play with.

Cancer

22 June – 22 July

Because Cancerians have no life of their own, they just love to hear about other people's problems – and they are gullible enough to think they might be of some help. How can they be when they have had no real experiences? They're supposed to be good home makers – this is a myth – but they've spread this rumour because they're just too scared to go into the real world and find out what it's like. They think they have exquisite taste – but their style is old-fashioned, dark and boring. They will get fat no matter what they eat.

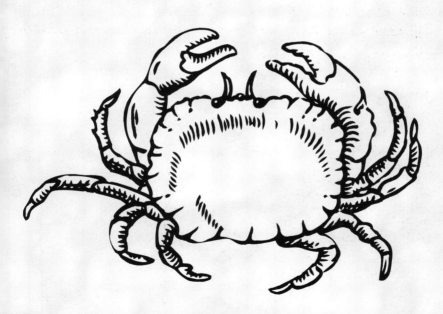

They think they have exquisite taste – but their style is old-fashioned, dark and boring

Personality

Their idea of a good night out is a dinner party – at their own house. Clinically they are agoraphobic although they invariably claim they are merely home-loving. They are the sign of the crab – do you want to know why? Because the sea that they live near is the perfect representation of their emotional state: wet, vast, capable of sinking pretty well anyone and unfathomable.

> *They are self-pitying, weak, pathetic, emotional limp rags. They wear their heart on their sleeves and by golly isn't it a wet one.*

Basically they are unstable, bordering slightly on the barking-mad. Not interesting-mad like Aquarians, or dangerous-mad like Scorpio, but scary-mad; you wouldn't want to be alone with one when they go off their trolleys. Think bunnies in boiling water, think a knife across your throat while you're sleeping.

you wouldn't want to be alone with one when they go off their trolleys

They are extremely clingy. Don't let them get too close or you'll regret it. They claim to be intuitive (they spy on people), protective (they smother people), cautious (they are afraid to take risks), excellent home-makers (agoraphobic), sympathetic listeners (they just want your gossip) and imaginative (no sense of reality).

Cancers are moody and will snap at you for no apparent reason. To get back in their good books you will have to ritually humiliate yourself, go down on bended knee and beg forgiveness, promising them you'll never do it again. And you'll never know what it was you did wrong. The reason for all this is they are simply control freaks. They want you uneasy, uncertain, afraid to put a foot wrong. They emotionally blackmail you to get whatever it is they want – and that can change from moment to moment – just to keep you on your toes. For Cancers life is one big drama and they just love to be theatrical, which probably explains why they go to the theatre so much.

Cancer in love

Oh what a wet mess they'll make of this. Cancer in love? You'll never hear the end of it when it comes to matters of the heart; they've met the right person or the wrong person; they've fallen in love at first sight, or after a long-term friendship; they've fallen for someone unsuitable, or completely suitable. I think they mistake us for someone who gives a damn. But still they'll go on about their love affairs, their broken heart or mended heart, their cute kids. It's all the same, emotional drivel.

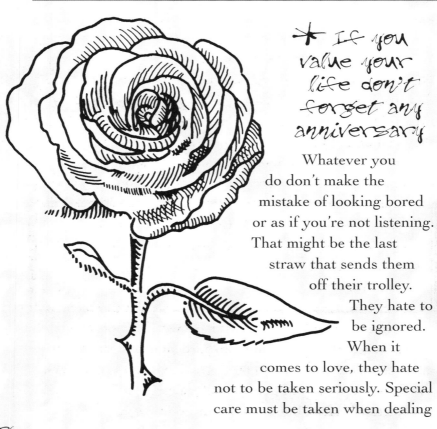

* If you value your life don't ~~forget~~ any anniversary

Whatever you do don't make the mistake of looking bored or as if you're not listening. That might be the last straw that sends them off their trolley. They hate to be ignored. When it comes to love, they hate not to be taken seriously. Special care must be taken when dealing with a Cancerian lover – you musn't mock them or tease them or poke fun at them. God forbid. They can't take a joke. They have no sense of humour and very little sense of fun.

They make a pretty big song and dance out of anything to do with love – soppy poetry, flowers, gifts. romantic locations, rings, tokens. body language, signals (conscious or unconscious, you've been warned) – and will stifle any sense of freedom, fresh air, time away from them, your own space, a day off, a night off or even daring to watch TV while they're talking to you. If you value your life don't forget any anniversary.

Cancer and sex

Now you'd expect them to be prudish, cautious, sensitive, delicate, discreet, straight-laced. No way. They are dirty little things. They keep their desires pretty quiet until they've hooked you and then they'll go berserk and expect you to perform all manner of bizarre and down-right deviant acts of sexual depravity.

> *They like to make love in chalets by the river, country house hotels, exotic hideaways. Once there. they will be busy taking notes on the décor while you're busy trying to satisfy their insatiable needs.*

Once the first flushes of lust have worn off for them they'll switch all their attention to gardening and leave you alone completely. Or they'll take up some bizarre sport such as tennis and insist you play as well instead of having sex. Completely bizarre, but that's a Cancerian for you.

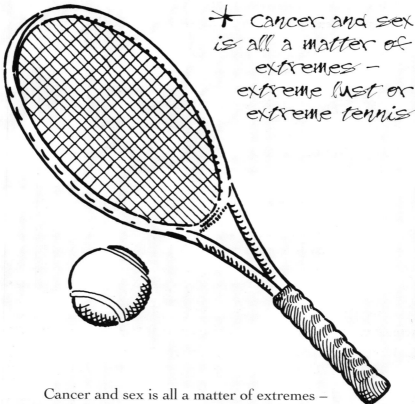

Cancer and sex is all a matter of extremes – extreme lust or extreme tennis

Cancer and sex is all a matter of extremes – extreme lust or extreme tennis. And you'll never know which so don't be getting any ideas, you'll be wrong.

Cancer in business

Cancerians works well if you give them lots of direction, orders, rules, rituals, things to fetch and carry – otherwise they are bossy, arrogant and self-opinionated. You can never tell which sort you're going to get before you employ them. And if you are unsatisfied you can't sack them – you'd ever hear the end of it, never stop them crying and clutching hankies.

If they work for themselves they are highly methodical, excessively neat, unbearably tidy, and organized. They colour code everything and make endless lists – they even have lists of their lists.

✱ They can earn quite a lot of money – all of which they spend on themselves or on their over-large brood of excessively cute kids

In business they do quite well servicing other people – organizing dinner parties, organising tours, massage parlours, counselling, that sort of thing. They actually do quite well in a funny sort of way. They can earn quite a lot of money – all of which they spend on themselves or on their over-large brood of excessively cute kids.

> *They often don't have to do any work at all as they marry rich spouses or inherit wealth or just find it in the street. They will never play the lottery as they think gambling beneath them. Their homes have too much velvet in them.*

Leo

23 July – 23 August

Ego first, second and last with a Leo. If only they'd stop to realize that the world doesn't quite revolve around them as much as they think it does. They are so full of themselves that others are taken in and they can build up quite a following of sycophants and hangers-on. This only helps bolster their already over-inflated sense of worth. They think any job they have is a career. They fail to notice how bad their lovers are because they're so busy watching their own performance – and that's what it is, a performance. They wear too much make-up.

Personality

> *They like to think that they are at their best in a noisy restaurant, being the centre of attraction, holding forth at the top of the table. But watch them slink away when its time to pay the bill. Not your most generous of signs this one. They bring white and drink red, and they drink far too much.*

Holding forth is probably their best position. They do love to tell everyone else what to think. They are bossy, dogmatic, opinionated and conceited. Trouble is, their opinions are always biased, subjective, unfair, based entirely on their own experiences, and short on facts. They have poor taste in clothes, as they think yesterday's fashions are still today's. Who'd have the nerve to tell them though?

✱ They do love to tell everyone else what to think. They are bossy, dogmatic, opinionated and conceited

And what is that thing they have about their hair? It is invariably messy, tangled and bushy and needs a good cut. They think they look like a lion, how wrong can you get?

They claim they only see the big picture, they paint on a wide canvas. They don't pay attention to detail. And do you know why? Lazy, that's why. They don't do detail because they can't be bothered. They are so stuck up they think the whole world revolves around them – there'll always be an underling to do the filing for them. They are distinctly below-average at everything. They know this and suffer terrible self-esteem problems. Good.

When they get old they get terribly depressed and make the mistake of thinking we care. They witter on about how much they could have done, how successful they once were. They progress to this stage as mutton dressed as lamb.

Their teeth are often yellow because they smoke too much and drink too much coffee.

✳ Their teeth are often yellow
because they smoke too much and
drink too much coffee

They won't go anywhere quietly. They can't sit through a play without talking or a film without being an unpaid highly vocal critic. They get shushed a lot in cinemas. Doesn't that tell you everything? They make bossy office managers.

Leo in love

What a showy little dog this one will turn out to be. A Leo in love, God protect us. This one will run and run – for about a week. You see the Leo is destined to be hurt in love, nay tortured, dismembered, torn apart. They bring it on themselves. If they could learn to keep their trap shut for five minutes they might just hang onto a lover. But they don't. They do love to change, to criticize, to tidy up, to argue with and finally, to drive away. It's in their nature. It's in the genes.

* Leo in love, God protect us. This one will run and run – for about a week

They fall in love with the most horribly unsuitable people; emotional cripples, too young, too old, too tall, too poor, already married (lots of this one), wrong gender, wrong planet.

They seek a white knight in shining armour who will rescue them from their current love affair which has invariably gone horribly wrong. Then when you do saddle up they'll play it all frosty and tell you that you've arrived at the wrong time, wrong place, or with the wrong colour armour, or that you've ridden the horse all wrong. You'd think they'd be grateful to have someone to be rescued by. Not a bit of it.

* They seek a white knight in shining armour who will rescue them, ~~from~~ their current love ~~affair~~ which has invariably gone horribly wrong

Leo and sex

They can be tigers or pussy cats, indifferent or over-demanding, turned off or turned on – you don't get any in-betweens with them. They are either ripping your clothes off or leaving them well alone. They either want sex ten times a night or not at all.

✱ They are either ripping your clothes off or leaving them, well alone

> They'll pounce on you when they're in the mood and get incredibly angry with you if you do the same. Best wait until you're asked. They like to think they are raunchy, daring, slightly dirty sorts of lovers. Truth is they are tame, boring and un-adventurous.

Their idea of a good night of sex is you worshipping them, looking after their needs, servicing them, satisfying them, performing for them. Notice anything missing there? Good, because they won't have.

Leo in business

Like the African lion that they are named after, they are fat and indolent, cowardly and very lazy. They think they are good at business but how could they possibly be? They have no staying power, no endurance, no money and no ideas.

✱ They have no staying power, no endurance, no money and no ideas

> *They like to run the show, but they lack any skills to do it. If only someone would tell them how bad they are at everything perhaps they'd go away and leave us to make some money. They make a lot of mistakes. All of which they try to cover up or blame someone else for.*

In business, as in everything else, they like to be in control. God knows why, they're hopeless at it all. They make lousy parents as well as lousy business people, entertainers, singers, dancers and PR people. They make good show-offs, though.

✳ *they like to be in control. God knows why, they're hopeless at it all*

If you are resolved to employ one make sure everything is nailed down or insured or replaceable or retrievable or expendable or disposable. They break stuff. They don't understand computers and cause them to crash. They deny this.

Virgo

24 August – 22 September

They have too many dictionaries and reference books. They could try reading a few of them. They are picky, sharp and bad-tempered if they don't get their own way. Their need for cleanliness and order is an obsession and they should consider therapy. They have few friends and those they do have, they criticize constantly. They have no emotions and might just as well be replaced by a machine. No one needs to wash their hands as much as they do.

Personality

The sign of Virgo is supposed to mean the virgin. Rubbish. The true sign of Virgo is a brick wall. They build barriers around themselves. Good. Let them rot behind them. Who wants to break down that wall to find an accountant lurking there? And that is invariably what you do find – accountants, number crunchers, computer geeks, button pushers, book–keepers and office managers. How boring.

Virgo and personality in the same sentence – that's an oxymoron. Does cash have soul? Do coins cry? Cut a bank statement and does it bleed? No, of course not. They lock their emotions away in money boxes and keep their feelings firmly between the pages of their cheque books. They have all the exhilaration of a filing cabinet.

✳ They lock their emotions away in money boxes and keep their ~~feelings firmly~~ between the pages ~~of~~ their cheque books

Virgoans are supposed to be discriminating, meticulous and tidy. The truth is they are just plain picky control freaks. Look inside their wardrobe. Have you ever seen anything so unnaturally neat? This is obsessive behaviour. In anyone else it would get you sectioned. They have too many jumpers.

> *Their idea of excitement is one glass of wine in a wine bar or a barbecue with a few friends — well four friends actually, always exactly four, never five or three, only four. It has to be neat and orderly. If they really want passion, excitement, daring, danger, they'll take a trip to a home furnishing store. They think wearing a paper hat at Christmas is terribly daring.*

They do have a problem with humour which seems to have got stuck somewhere around the school playground level. They are surprisingly coarse and like nothing better than jokes about people being sick or going to the lavatory. For some strange reason they seem to think this is funny. It might just be because they never do such things themselves. It wouldn't suit their image to be seen doing bodily functions. In an ideal world they wouldn't even eat, which is surprising when you see how many of them become fat.

They are fussy, obsessional and hypercritical hypochondriacs. They like to break in rather than break out. They always seek conformity and traditional values. They like to fit in, to belong, to blend in. They have far too many cushions and too many gadgets in their kitchen.

✴ They like to break in rather than break out

Virgo in love

> *They are over-concerned when in love and will need constant reassurance. You have to tell them how much you love them every twenty minutes without fail or they will feel threatened and lacking in self-esteem. They need constant reassurance that every thing is perfect in their little perfect worlds. Wipe down the kitchen surfaces a lot if you want them to feel loved.*

Cute, sickly, passionless, adorable, and sweet. That's your Virgo in love for you – sickly-sweet. Golden syrup-sweet. They like to hold hands with their intended, a lot, far too much. They giggle and bat their eyelids and that sort of thing. They like to feed their lover and do helpful things for them like putting toothpaste on their toothbrushes. Being in love for a Virgo means having someone to tidy up, smarten up, look after. They don't need a lover, they need a child. They like to look at magazines a lot – especially glossy ones to help you plan your wedding, or re-decorate your home.

✱ They don't need a lover, they need a child

Once they have got their ideal partner – and don't worry if you aren't, they'll soon mould you to fit – they set about altering your eating habits. They do like their organics and their faddy diets and their over-sweet drinks. Nothing too grown up for them, so forget a decent steak or a bottle of beer. They drink herbal teas, so if you want to make a really big impression on them suggest a cup of hot water, that'll get them.

Virgo and sex

If you like going to bed surrounded by teddy bears and
stuffed animals you'll do fine. If you like quick clean sex
you'll be fine. If you like anything out of the ordinary, sexy,
adventurous, or fun, then you're going to be very unhappy
I'm afraid. Sex for the Virgo is a bit like going swimming.
It's all cold and clean and a bit wet. You'll need a good rub
down and a shower afterwards and it's all so healthy, so
unbelievably healthy. And no, you can't lie there afterwards
having a cigarette – heaven forbid.

✱ If you
like going
to bed
surrounded
by teddy
bears and
stuffed
animals
you'll do
fine

And boy do they like routine. Touch this bit first, do this next, follow up with this. Each and every time. You'll get no surprises here. You'll stick to the script or they'll sulk – boy are they good at that. They don't like spontaneous sex either. You'll do it at the right and proper time, once a week, in the right temperature controlled circumstances. No out of door sex for the Virgo, or being cold or sweaty or taken by sudden passion. They have lots of inhibitions.

✱ *You'll stick to the script or they'll sulk – boy are they good at that*

Oh yes, you'd better be good at it. They can be very picky lovers. Make sure you wash first, lots of nice smells – they don't really like bodies so be clean and hygienic. Keep your bedroom spotless and make sure there's lots of tissues, they like tissues. They don't like to eat in bed, too many crumbs.

Virgo in business

Imagine your tax inspector and you have pretty well your perfect Virgo. A busybody. A stickler for rules and regulations. They would make a good car park attendant – 'You can't park there'. Do you get the picture?

How many times can you say accountant? That's it really. Anything without excitement, danger, hard work, responsibility, creativity or free thinking. They make good food hygiene inspectors – busy poking about in other people's fridges. They don't like to be in charge and would much rather be told what to do – and have lots of rules. They do like rules.

✳ They make good ~~food~~ hygiene inspectors – busy poking about in other people's ~~fridges~~

Remember those lovely old films set in hospitals with the big bosomy matron – that's your Virgo that is. Bossy, highly-organized, scary, intimidating, neat. They like to smell of carbolic soap. They never go into business on their own unless it is to set up a secretarial school where they turn out neat little Virgos in neat little business suits.

When they aren't at work they are restless little people who like dull activities like shopping, gardening, or walking. They like to be busy. Trouble is, they like everyone around them to be busy as well, you don't get away with anything. They make good slave drivers.

Libra

23 September – 23 October

Librans think of themselves as balanced and able to weigh up both sides – in actual fact they are ditherers with no real opinions or beliefs. They think they are quite artistic, but most people see them as wishy-washy and indecisive with no grip on reality. Quite right too. They are cowardly and incapable of standing up to anyone or anything. They would make a good professional yes-person.

Personality

> *Like their opposite sign – Aries – they do like to do most of their thinking below their belts. They really can only relate on a sexual level and consequently they think sex is love, and love is sex. They are very, very flirtatious.*

They always appear to have been born with a silver spoon in their mouth – drifting through life without ever having a proper job and somehow surviving nonetheless. They do engender a great deal of jealousy because of this, especially from members of their own sex, whereas those of the opposite sex just want to look after them and be seduced by them. They end up being mothered or murdered.

✳ *they do like to do most of their thinking below their belts*

If wall paper had opinions then Libra would steal them. They don't have a single original idea of their own but instead will nick them from anyone around them – and then claim them as their own. They are also very gullible, so you can implant false opinions in them and then stand back and watch the fun as they set out to convince everyone that what they say is true.

✳ *They don't have a single original idea of their own but instead will nick them from anyone around them*

They tend to think the height of intellectual stimulation is a garden party – preferably one with royalty present. They see a challenging job as being an actor or dancer – one-man band would be a little taxing for them. Now don't get me wrong, I'm not saying your typical Libra is shallow, but a sheet of paper has more depth than they do. They are frivolous, changeable, superficial and idealistic. The idea of 3D has never entered their pretty little heads.

They are terribly petty and they spend far too much time decorating their home. They have a weakness for all things sweet and sickly. They eat too many tea cakes.

✳ They have a weakness for all things sweet and sickly

> *Librans are supposed to be balanced individuals – but the reason why they can't make decisions is not because they are busy weighing up the pros and cons, but because they are too lazy to think about such things. Ask them if they want tea or coffee and you throw their minds into a complete spin.*

Mind you they are always cheerful and optimistic – even when running up huge debts, causing deep and lasting hurt in their personal relationships, and failing to deal with any of life's real problems. They have only one thought – me, me, me. Of all the astrological signs they are the most selfish, the most self-centred, the most narcissistic, egotistical and arrogant. The think they can charm people and carry it off, but they are hurtful and oblivious of other people's feelings. They spend too much time looking in mirrors.

✳ They spend too much time
looking in mirrors

Libra in love

They will tell you that they are great lovers, and that everyone falls in love with them at the drop of a hat. Unfortunately, a lot of silly people do exactly that. They seem to attract shallow people to them. Anyone with a hint of substance or strength would run a mile from these fops and vane dandies. We are still all jealous of them, despite all this, because everything seems to come to them so easily, without them having to do any work. They also always have the best people on their arm.

They are complete lounge lizards and will cheerfully secure, love, and leave any willing victim who crosses their path. A Libran would do anything, or anyone, who would give them house room.

If you should be so unfortunate – or shallow enough – to fall in love with a Libra, then you will spend a lot of time waiting for them to come home; they'll be off making goo goo eyes at someone else. They have the morals of a rat and the ethics of a guttersnipe.

* They have the morals of a rat and the ethics of a guttersnipe

They aren't really sure what love is. They think they know, but they are so vapid that they don't have any real feelings. Anything as strong as love leaves them out in the cold – they don't experience it because it is too deep for them. Mind you some puddles are too deep for them as well.

Libra and sex

Lustful creatures, disgusting little beasts. They think with their groins. They believe copulation is the answer to all of life's problems. In fact, the only problem they are prepared to consider is where their next sexual encounter is coming from – that's the limit of their intellectual and reasoning powers.

* Lustful creatures, disgusting little beasts. They think with their groins

> *They like dark bedrooms lit with candles and lots of satin furnishings – everything has to be totally decadent, totally over-the-top, and totally overblown. They like to have sex with lots of mirrors around – this isn't for your benefit. They also like to play tacky classical music because they think it makes them seem intellectual.*

Mind you, in bed they are pretty good – they'll tell you just how good they are if you ask. In fact, even if you don't ask, they will still tell you. If they want to seduce you they will turn on all their charm – which, to be fair, is considerable – but this only lasts until you take your clothes off. Then they lose interest. You will be dismissed as yesterday's toy. They will use and abuse you and then cast you aside as soon as the novelty has worn off – about five minutes after they have finished. They love waving goodbye to ex-lovers.

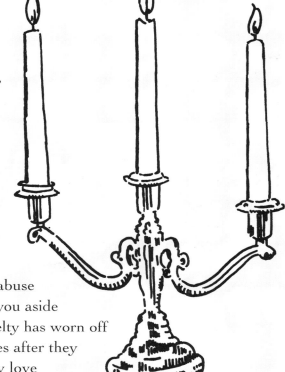

Libra in business

Ha, there's an oxymoron if I ever heard one – Libra in business. Libra in sloth, libra in laziness, libra in indolence, that sounds more like it. They have all the aptitude and capacity for work, and earning money as a chimp has for typing Shakespeare.

✳ They really shouldn't ever gamble, they always lose

If they do have to have a job then they'll opt for something easy, stylish and decadent which allows them to display their charm – a fashion designer or beautician, or an actor or art dealer.

> *They don't do self-employment, entrepreneuring, or partnerships – unless they're the sleeping partner – or any work that requires effort, thinking, or forward-planning. They really shouldn't ever gamble, they always lose.*

They don't make great leaders – they don't even make lousy ones. They are far better at foppishness, dandyism, daintiness and dilettantism. They have no idea of time so are constantly late which irritates everyone, but the Libra thinks it only adds to their charm. If only they could see themselves as other people do. They have no smart clothes.

Scorpio

24 October – 22 November

Scorpios are disruptive and cruel – and they like it that way. They spent their childhood pulling the wings off flies and now they feel hampered and restricted because they can't do it as an adult. So they just go out of their way to irritate everyone around them. They like offending people and have no social graces whatsoever. They may well end up being assassinated. They are very argumentative.

Personality

> They have lots and lots of really powerful emotions. Ones which would tear us apart. Scorpio instead thrives on them – they are all feelings of murder. Scorpio is a magnet for weak and unstable people. They collect weirdos, oddballs, wackoes and loonies – anyone they can control, torture, inflict pain on and generally abuse.

✳ Scorpio is a magnet for weak and unstable people

If you want a spy or an assassin, or an industrial espionage expert, then get yourself one of these. They won't let you down. They can steal, kill, pillage and all with a smile. And whatever they do they'll surprize you. They hate routine, and will go out of their way to be unconventional, inventive and wacky. They like to be seen as rebellious, debonair and suave. They are simply unpleasant and cruel.

✳ They can steal, kill, pillage and all with a smile

They don't like to be bored. If they are allowed to get bored then they can become quite spiteful. Out of this spitefulness comes a truly unpleasant and sadistic nature that revels in preying on the weak, the vulnerable and the defenceless – they like to inflict pain on helpless little creatures. Unfortunately, that means the rest of us.

> *They make bad enemies so don't cross them. If they combine this enmity with criminal acts you have one of the most dangerous and ruthless gang leaders ever. But they will dress well and always have exquisitely polished shoes to do their kicking with.*

They have terrible taste in art. They furnish their homes with too much red and black. They like to think this looks contemporary and cool. Instead it looks sinister and macabre. Don't tell them this, they would think that was cool.

They are not good team players – too much resentment, and jealousy. Better to let them run their own business, however dubious that may be.

✳ they like to inflict pain on helpless little creatures. Unfortunately, that means the rest of us

Scorpio in love

, I don't want to be unpleasant but Scorpio in love is
ething I don't want to think about, let alone write about.
It is simply too dark, too dirty, too close to the knuckle.
They don't have the same respect for the law as the rest of
us and will happily commit every sexual taboo going, and a
few that haven't been invented yet.

**✳ It is simply too dark, too dirty,
too close to the knuckle**

> *I'm not sure they are capable of falling in love. Falling in lust,
> yes, but love? I don't think so. To fall in love you need a heart.
> They have a lump of ice there instead. Think James Bond here.
> Would he fall in love? Of course not. He'd have sex and then
> shoot them. That's the perfect love affair for a Scorpio.*

If they do fall in love with you then they will expect to
own you, control you, possess and dominate you. They like
to play complicated role-playing games – mostly where you
have to wear tight restrictive clothes. If you like this slave-
master relationship you will be very happy, just as long as
you realize you will always be the slave. Well, that is until
they tire of you. Most slaves would get dismissed but Scorpio
will have you shot instead.

**✳ They like to play complicated
role-playing games**

Scorpio and sex

Dark, dangerous, mad, and sadistic. I once knew someone who wanted to sleep with a Scorpio and they asked me what sort of gift they should give them to make a good impression. I suggested a silk scarf. They duly bought one and it worked; the Scorpio tied them up and had their wicked way with them. And left them tied up! Now that's really nasty.

If you are going to sleep with a Scorpio make sure you are fit and have endurance and stamina. They have super-human strength and will like to make love for very long periods of time. They like doing it in public places, like cinemas. They would do it in the street if they thought it would make them more alluring.

✳ They would do it in the street if they thought it would make them more alluring

As for what goes on in a Scorpio bedroom I don't want to know. You go there but don't tell me. They do make jealous lovers though, so don't be unfaithful to them. If anyone is going to be unfaithful it will be them. They are even unfaithful to the ones they are being unfaithful with. If you do betray them – or they think you have – they will seek revenge. You will pay for it , and pay in blood and pain.

Scorpio in business

If you go into business with one of these you'll get burnt. They are pretty ruthless. Employ one if you want a salesperson who will stop at nothing to make their targets.

They are capable of studying hard but I would keep a very close eye on them – they are rather too fond of bizarre chemistry and do seem to be addicted to the poison cupboard.

✷ they are rather ~~too fond~~ of bizarre chemistry and do seem to be addicted to the poison cupboard

Scorpios are passionate people and like their work to reflect this. If they do have a 'normal' job it will be one where they can work in the background and still be the star – a research scientist or an inventor. Just don't expect them to invent or discover anything that benefits mankind.

If they have to have a career, and frankly they would rather inherit their wealth – then they do well in any field that involves secrets – a psychiatrist, a detective (think Sherlock Holmes),or even an undertaker. They do the dark and unsavoury jobs none of the rest of us would want to.

Sagittarius

23 November – 21 December

Sagittarians have no real talent or skills and survive purely on gut instinct and luck. They are a status-seeking snob with a reckless risk-taking approach to life – which seems to pay off, for the moment (but their day is coming). They really care what other people think of them – how pathetic. They love travel, but it's really only running away for them, isn't it? Anything to avoid an honest days work.

Personality

> *The symbol of Sagittarius is a centaur firing a bow and arrow –*
> *strange or what? Half-human, half-horse, with six limbs. And*
> *what are they shooting at? No one knows, no one cares. Actually*
> *they are a bit ordinary and the only thing extraordinary about*
> *them is that they have this silly symbol. Yes, that's it. A silly*
> *symbol and they dine out on that.*

The truth is, they don't have much of a personality. They
are a bit like cotton wool. You know its there. You know it
has a purpose. But that's about it. You couldn't have a
conversation with cotton wool would you? Or a meaningful
relationship. Or give it a job.

✳ The truth is, they don't have
   much of a personality

They always think they have some hidden talent – be it
writing, composing music, singing or dancing – and that it
won't take long for fame and fortune to come their way.
They end up blaming everyone else for not being discovered.
It never occurs to them that we looked under their rock and
deemed them talentless and undiscoverable – we passed
them by.

✳ It never occurs to them
that we looked under their rock
   and deemed them talentless
      and undiscoverable

> *You get two types of Sagittarius – the quiet depressed hermit-type and the pompous, knowledgeable, know-it-all type. They both think that their way is the right way and that the rest of us are out of step with them.*

They love hanging out in big gatherings where they think they're the centre of attention. They actually blend rather nicely into the wallpaper, but don't tell them. They think snowboarding and juggling are subjects for worthy conversation as they are a bit vacant upstairs, although they do a nice line in pretend philosophy. Truth is they would rather get back to watching TV.

★ They think snowboarding and juggling are subjects for worthy conversation

For such a pallid, limp sign they sure have big egos. Understandable for some signs – you expect Leo to be arrogant and proud and cocksure – but not little Sagittarius. From them you would expect quietude, modesty and humility. Instead you get a giant chip on the shoulder, arrogance and sneering condescension. They think the world owes them a living, a roof over their head and lots of money. We owe them nothing.

✶ They think the world owes them a living, a roof over their head and lots of money. We owe them nothing

Sagittarius in love

It doesn't happen a lot – it could be all that arrogance – but when it does the earth moves. Well it shimmers a little. They fall in love with totally unsuitable people – the kind who will prop up their egos and pander to their aches and pains – they are all terrible hypochondriacs and suffer endless twinges, joint pains, muscular aches, sprains strains and tendon pulls.

✶ they are all terrible hypochondriacs

They aren't terribly demonstrative and their lover will complain of a lack of affection, romance, sensitivity and tactile companionship – a Sagittarius don't touch much. They do, however, liked to be touched, a lot. Perhaps because they are a little touched in the head?

Their idea of romance is to send their lover a postcard from some exotic place they have fled to. They often travel alone because no one else will go with them, and not because they prefer it. They are always talking of where they have been and where they are going to go – it could be enough to put anyone off but, surprisingly, they do seem to be able to attract love attention.

✱ They often travel alone because no one else will go with them

They are often very thin – they think it makes themselves look more interesting – and their choice of partner borders on the, well, how shall we say it? ...fat. Yes, they like a big'un. Nice, well-rounded, with lots of meat on the bone. Something to get their teeth into, something to hang onto. I think it reminds them of their mother.

Sagittarius and sex

They relate to beds as places to sleep. Because they like to lie in bed all day if they can get away with it, the idea of using such a warm and comfortable hideaway for sex is slightly repugnant to them. Why waste all that effort when you could be using that time to sleep some more?

Once you get them into bed they are simply hopeless lovers. They value speed over everything, including experience, flare, prowess, technique and a loving touch.

✶ Once you get them into bed they are simply hopeless lovers

If you got one alone on an exotic beach complete with sunshine, warmth and indolence you might get them to show an interest – but I doubt it. They're more likely to be dreaming of even more exotic places – and running away again.

Sagittarius in business

The very idea of working is so repugnant, so horrific that I'm afraid to even mention it. Of course, and this is between you and me, they think they work hard because they spend so much time locked up in their own heads, but in the meantime they haven't actually lifted a finger.

If they do have a job they'll find a million ways to shirk their duties. They usually come up with a good line in fictitious illnesses, aches and pains, and unprovable headaches. They phone in sick so often their employer forgets they were ever employed in the first place. They are simply monstrously lazy.

✷ *They phone in sick so often their employer ~~forgets~~ they were ever employed in the ~~first~~ place*

They let money slip through their fingers when they are young and then either take to hoarding it or borrowing it off friends and family. They either save everything or nothing – no grey areas for them – so you get a spendthrift or a miser.

> *They have trouble getting decent jobs because they flunked so much at school. They often work for organisations that don't worry too much about qualifications – who are just glad to get a body to man the phones, the stand, the pumps – such as charities and mental health institutions, petrol stations and hot dog stands.*

Capricorn

22 December – 20 January

One day a Capricorn will take a risk and the world will stop in shock. They are cool to the point of frozen; self-possessed to the point of wooden; and sceptical to the point of not even believing in themselves. They are the old-fashioned type – stuck in another era, another time warp. They are staid and boring, tight-fisted and mean. They have no true emotions. They have no real sex life.

Personality

> Capricorn is the sign of the goat — wild, capricious and at home on the mountainside. Rubbish. Capricorn is really the sign of the crocodile — dangerous, predatory and mean. They like to make money, make some more money and finally make a bit more just in case. They lavish any emotional life they have on their finances.

✳ They lavish any emotional life they have on their finances

They are a cold-blooded reptile — ambitious, ruthless, determined and cunning. They look ahead and upwards and plot how to get there. They never worry about keeping up with the Jones's, they *are* the Jones's. They like you to know how much they are worth, what their house is worth, and what their car cost.

✳ They are a cold-blooded reptile — ambitious, ruthless, determined and cunning

They aren't very people-orientated and can come across as distant, aloof and somewhat disapproving. They do like people to hero worship them though, it makes them feel superior. They need to spend a bit more time outdoors as their skin is a bit pasty. They could also do with looking at themselves from behind in a decent full-length mirror.

They like to hoard, and fear having their savings being taken from them – all this wealth could be stolen, the markets could crash, there could be a run on the bank. They lie awake at night listing all the things that could go wrong. Consequently they do like to invest in burglar alarms.

> *They are very serious and like nothing better than serious discussions – about the exchange rate, the run on the currency, the bank's interest rates and how much to invest in coffee beans.*

✱ They lie awake at night
listing all the things that
could go wrong

In their thinking they have all the flexibility of a steel rod – you try getting one to change their mind. They are a fixed sign – fixed in thought, word and deed. They do nothing spontaneously. If it hasn't been diaried then they won't do it. They do like order – in fact they make the Virgo seem positively reckless and messy. They are supposed to have a very dry sense of humour – never seen a sign of it myself. They are miserly, dour, pessimistic and a bit of a wet blanket. They are fastidious about germs – Howard Hughes was a Capricorn, no surprizes there then.

Capricorn in love

What a depressing thought. A goat in love. How very sad.
They have all the passion of two people watching TV, and
no doubt they would watch some dreary programme on the
stock market. They like to sit on sofas drinking tea
together in matching cardigans. They like slippers.

You would think they were shy seeing as how tongue-
tied they seem, unable to speak in the presence of the
opposite sex, looking at the floor, all that shuffling from foot
to foot. But shy they are not. They are just so robotic that
they don't have emotional responses. That's why they try to

appear shy, it's a cover up for the fact that they don't know how to be, or how to act when confronted with emotion.

✳ *They are just so robotic that they don't have emotional responses*

> *They don't do romance or trivia or small-talk or baby-talk or endearments. They do serious. They do ponderous. They do weighty. Falling in love with one of these is a bit like falling in love with a rhinoceros – heavy, grey ... and horny.*

Capricorn and sex

The one area in which the Capricorn lets their hair down is in the bedroom. They do like their sex. In fact they can be a bit like the proverbial pig at a trough. These are very private people who don't like being asked what they are thinking or what they are feeling, but take their clothes off and they lose all inhibitions. They won't take their own clothes off, mind – they don't initiate anything – so you'll have to set the ball rolling. Once you do they'll surprize you with their stamina – and exhaust you with their energy. They don't have a great deal of finesse but by golly they have staying power.

✳ *take their clothes ~~off~~ and they lose all inhibitions*

If you like being wooed, flirted with, seduced, romanced and teased, better find another playmate; Capricorn are direct and blunt.

> *They do like one lover at a time and preferably a long-term one No one-night-stands for them. They are faithful to the point of boring, they don't even commit adultery in their heads. When it comes down to it, all a Capricorn wants to do is play good old-fashioned missionaries.*

Capricorn in business

Plod, plod, plod. That's a Capricorn thinking out loud. They make great bankers, and can be found lurking in the basements of big grey buildings, working on their numbers.

Give them a task and they'll relentlessly trawl their way through it until it is done. Give them a challenge or an idea or a new thing and they'll be hopelessly lost. This is not the brightest button in the box. This is not the sharpest of knives in the kitchen drawer. Sure they can follow an instruction manual – they're brilliant at putting flat pack furniture together or making model aircrafts – but they do get a bit lost if you ask them to think for themselves. Now I'm not saying they're stupid – far from it – but a bit slow? Yes, that's it. A bit slow. You can, however, trust them, they don't have the wits to steal from you.

✱ This is not the brightest button in the box

At work they are serious and always on time. They do occasionally make jokes which throws people completely, mainly because they don't expect it and because the jokes are so terrible – their sense of humour is sadly lacking. Their sense of timing is awry. Their story-telling abilities are non-existent. But don't tell them – they think they are brilliantly funny.

Aquarius

21 January – 19 February

Aquarians really ought to care a little more about who they sleep with – especially in this day and age. They are laid-back, organized and cool – these are also the attributes of any good confidence trickster. They never appear to do any work but they always have plenty of money – they must be sponging off someone. They are lazy and indulgent. They could try repaying some of their debts some time. They hate cuddly toys.

Personality

> *They are the most stubborn sign in the zodiac and would willingly go to the gallows rather than have to admit they were wrong, lose face, back down, or compromise. They make a stand about things we would consider trivial. You won't beat them. Give it up now.*

✱ They are the most stubborn sign in the zodiac and would willingly go to the gallows rather than have to admit they were wrong

Again and again and again the word 'barking' crops up whenever anyone is describing this most unorthodox of signs. And barking is what they are. They may look pretty normal but inside there is an alien's brain.

Aquarians make good Zen monks as they already march to the sound of one hand clapping. They are stoic and feel no pain nor cold nor discomfort. Trouble is they expect everyone else to put up with such harsh conditions and look down on you if you do feel cold or hungry or tired. They are driven, determined, ruthless zealots and fanatics. They are, in fact, quite utterly insane.

✱ They are driven, determined, ruthless zealots and fanatics. They are, in fact, quite utterly insane

> *Leave them to get on with their own private world and just serve them, obey them, worship them and devote yourself to them and they will be entirely happy. They won't of course reward you, talk to you or notice you, but this does not matter. You will be serving a higher life form.*

They don't answer when you speak to them because they are so wrapped up in their plans, their dreams, their schemes that they can't be bothered with the likes of a petty earthling. They eat and sleep to a different pattern to the rest of us. They like to feel cold when we enjoy being warm. They don't keep normal hours.

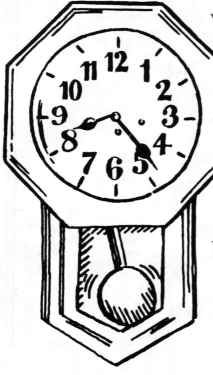

You will never understand what makes them tick, even if you live to be a hundred. They don't tick like us. If we tick they tock. They march to another drumbeat entirely, one that is playing inside their head and no one else can hear, not even other Aquarians. They are unique – and who would want any more of them?

* *They don't tick like us. If we tick they tock*

Aquarius in love

> *If you are unlucky enough to fall for one of these then you aren't going to be wooed or romanced or wined and dined much. You will however get lectured, pontificated at, talked down to and patronized.*

What? Are you mad? You think these people fall in love with human beings? Oh, come on. Haven't you leant anything about them yet? They fall in love with laboratory specimens, chemical compounds, spiders, toads, entire solar systems, books, research projects – but people? Never. Well, not individuals.

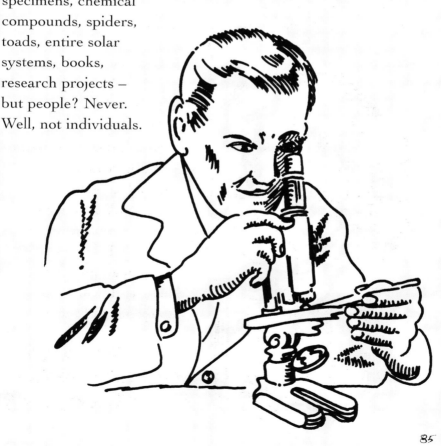

They do love family and society and the whole of mankind. But not on a one-to-one basis, far too close, too feely, too embarrassing.

And if you do ever manage to get an Aquarius up the aisle you'll find yourself married to someone who never says 'I love you', shows any affection or even lives with you – kissing may also be considered unhygienic. They may take off on research projects on the other side of the world but they won't be around to put out the garbage or do the school run.

Aquarius and sex

You'd better get used to being examined, researched and dissected. Spontaneous? Yes. Exciting? Yes, sometimes. Educational? Always – you might end up having sex on a trampoline or in a reference library or in a dancing school – all those places you wouldn't normally associate with being sexy will be explored with an Aquarius as a lover.

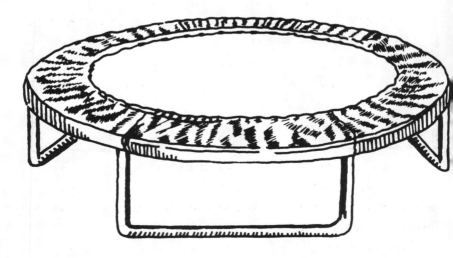

They think everything from falling in love, to sex to work, can be collated, programmed, pre-set, pinholed and encoded in a computer printout. They firmly believe that if you break things down into their smallest part you will understand them. Of course, an Aquarius will never understand the bits marked 'feelings' or 'emotions'.

✳ *Of course, an Aquarius will never understand the bits marked 'feelings' or 'emotions'*

The one good thing about them is that they tend to remain faithful. They may be aloof and detached but when it comes to love this does not translate into straying or flirting (they wouldn't know how) or having one-night-stands (they will all do this one once just to see what it is like – more research you see).

Aquarius in business

They like to wear white coats and stethoscopes and have lots of pens in their top pocket, so that they are always ready to make notes on any bizarre behaviour they may observe. Their watches always have lots of dials and time zones and are waterproof right down to the bottom of the deepest ocean.

Not your great entrepreneur or business person. They can't do paperwork or detail or even turn up on time. But give them a decent science lab and they'll produce a cure for cancer or design an interstellar rocket ship powered by thought or hot air or paperclips. The normal, decent, well-paid job is not for them. They like to be underwater palaeontologists, astrologers, radiographers. Think vintage. Think black-and-white. Think science. Think in terms of radio rather than DVDs and you'll understand Aquarius in business.

They are small boys looking at ants with a magnifying glass and wondering why so many of them spontaneously burst into flames on a hot summer's day. They are obsessed with the past and love nothing better than digging up tombs, graves, archaeological sites, bones, dinosaurs, and incriminating evidence.

* They are small boys looking at ants with a magnifying glass and wondering why so many of them spontaneously burst into flames on a hot summer's day

Pisces

20 February – 20 March

Pisceans have a vivid imagination and sense of drama. They frequently suffer from conspiracy delusions of being followed. They are good actors which makes it hard for people to get to know them – a fact they like because it makes them seem enigmatic and mysterious. They like people to regard them as a lot deeper than they really are.

Personality

> *They follow anything to do with the New Age but have no real interest – it's all just an excuse to seduce people and get them to take their clothes off.*

Because Pisceans operate entirely on an emotional level all their emotions are honed to a point of rawness the rest of us couldn't live with. They experience the pain of jealousy and resentment more intensely than we do. They hurt when you betray them – and betray them you will. They ask for it.

✳ *it's all just an excuse to seduce people and get them to take their clothes* ~~off~~

They bear a grudge forever. They are always suspecting their partner of having an affair. Naturally if you get accused sufficiently then you might as well do it; Pisceans drive their lovers to adultery just so they can be proved right.

Because of this jealousy they'll check your phone bills, trawl through your garbage and spy on your every movement. They judge you by their own standards.

✳ *Pisceans drive their lovers to adultery just so they can be proved right*

Pisceans are scruffy little devils and they have an odd idea of personal hygiene – check their teeth if you don't believe me. They are vague about plans and diary dates and can drive you mad with their seeming casual attitude to life. They are careless and lose keys, and books – especially precious ones you've foolishly leant them. They like you to think of them as cool and carefree, but they are just messy, selfish and disorganized.

✳ *Pisceans are scruffy little devils and they have an odd idea of personal hygiene*

As for the practicalities of life, well you might as well give up on them now. They collect parking tickets, fail to remember to tax their car every year, miss all the important anniversaries, forget to set the timer on the video machine and they break all electrical gadgets. But ask them to talk about themselves and they seem to spring instantly to life.

Pisceans in love

You'd think them terribly prudish when you first meet them but they will beguile and seduce you, lead you astray and do it with such charm you'll have taken your kit off before you know it. They are also pretty indecisive so they can't get rid of any lover.

> *If however they ever get ditched by a lover then the floodgates open. Not that they really care, not deep down inside, but they do like to show off their emotional side and will blub on anyone's shoulder; they feel if they fake a real emotion, such as grief, they might actually feel something. This is doubtful.*

People who have Pisceans for lovers often feel crushed by them because they can be taken up and then suddenly dropped for no reason. But again, this is part of their power play. By keeping you unsettled they think you'll want more – treat 'em mean and keep 'em keen. It usually just leaves you feeling worthless and dirty. Then again you might like this.

> ✱ It usually just leaves you ~~feeling worthless and dirty.~~ Then again you might like this

Pisceans and sex

Pisceans don't need sex, they need power. They like getting you naked so you'll feel vulnerable and they feel in control. The sad thing is, they do tend to be able to get more people naked than any other sign. They'll use whatever tactics it takes – offering a massage, aromatherapy, artistic photos –

you name it. They may even offer to work out your astrology chart for you – you would of course have to be naked for them to do this.

> *They think themselves quite the sexpert and have studied tantric sex in some depth. Truth is they are a bit quick. Don't for heavens sake mention it; they have terribly frail egos and can't take any criticism at all. If you want to escape from their bizarre power games all you have to do is laugh at their private bits.*

They do like to be very secretive in their sexual relationships, expecting you to reveal all your fantasies, past lovers, sexual preferences, while they nod wisely and give absolutely nothing away about themselves. Their whole motivating force is power.

Knowledge is power – they think that if they give nothing away you won't have any power over them. They can also be a bit lax in their personal habits – they can't be trusted to own a bar of soap – which makes going to bed with a Pisces a bit of a gamble. They may have showered, but then again, they may not have.

Their bedrooms are always a mess and if they look tidy then look under the bed and you'll find where they shoved everything five minutes before you arrived. They collect lovers, so be prepared to share. They think of this as free-love, liberated and modern. In reality it is tacky and unhygienic. Again this is as a power thing – the more the merrier – and they like to lure people from the straight and narrow into some pretty weird threesomes, partner swapping, and ten-in-a-hot-tub gatherings.

> ✱ They think of this as free-love, liberated, modern. In reality it is tacky and unhygienic

Pisces in business

They don't do business, or jobs really. There's no motivation for them. There's no easy way to get people to take their clothes off. They'd do much better to enter a career as a counsellor, doctor, nurse, or hypnotist. They will work in any situation that puts them in charge and you at a disadvantage. They like to be knowledgeable about things so that you feel inferior, and grateful to them for any knowledge they dole out.

They claim to love art but in reality they like looking at smutty pictures. They claim to love dancing, but it's really just an excuse to grip you a little too tightly. They will never make any money as their motives are always suspect, but boy will they be jealous if you do have any success.

Let's put it this way. Always ask the shoe shop assistant what star sign they are, and if they are Pisces then back out slowly. They will sell you shoes that are unsuitable, pinch, too expensive, the wrong style and wrong purpose – and the whole time they'll be massaging your toes and looking up your skirt or trouser leg.

✳ *they'll be massaging your toes and looking up your skirt or trouser leg*

They do need to work for themselves and preferably alone as they aren't too good at spending time with other people – this might have something to do with their hygiene problems. If you do give them a job they'll turn out to be trouble-makers, sowing seeds of discontent and muttering in dark corners. They like to organize strikes.

Acknowledgements

The author, Richard MacDonald, would like to thank the Parker twins for their invaluable contribution to the world of astrology over so many years. He also acknowledges the brilliant work of Jonathan Cainer, who has always been such an inspiration.